Upper Canada Village

Photographs by John de Visser
Introduction by William J. Patterson

Toronto
Oxford University Press
1981

CANADIAN CATALOGUING IN PUBLICATION DATA

De Visser, John, 1930-
    Upper Canada Village

ISBN 0-19-540363-0 (bound)

1. Upper Canada Village (Ont.) – Description –
Views. 2. Historic sites – Ontario – Upper Canada
Village – Pictorial works. I. Patterson, William J.
(William John), 1930-   II. Title.

FC3065.U66D48   917.13'75   C81-094122-8
F1057.8.D48

© Oxford University Press (Canadian Branch) 1981

ISBN 0-19-540363-0

1 2 3 4 - 4 3 2 1

Printed in Hong Kong
EVERBEST PRINTING COMPANY LIMITED

Introduction
by William J. Patterson

Upper Canada Village, near Morrisburg, Ont., is an outdoor historical museum composed of transplanted and restored buildings grouped in the form of a rural village typical of eastern Upper Canada before Confederation. An interpretative device, it is intended to provide 'a living monument to the way of life of Upper Canada's earliest settlers'. It is a tribute to its creators that to the millions of visitors who have walked its dusty (or, depending on the weather, muddy) streets, the village is very real, conveying vividly and intimately the sights and sounds and smells—the very feeling—of village life more than a century ago.

Ontario, formerly called Upper Canada, owes its beginnings partly to the thousands of displaced American refugees—'Loyalists'—who remained loyal to the 'Unity of the Empire'. Upper Canada Village was laid out on farm land originally belonging to Loyalists—Sergeant Loucks and Private Hickey of the King's Royal Regiment of New York—and five of the principal buildings have Loyalist origins. The Village is situated on the banks of the St Lawrence River, which is the dominant presence. The connecting thread of so much Canadian history, the river is a constant reminder of the time when it was the great water highway for French and British explorers, missionaries, soldiers, settlers, merchants, and fur traders, leading them into the heart of the continent. Rapids impeded navigation in the upper river until eight canals were built to bypass them in the eighteenth and nineteenth centuries. A mammoth expansion of this route to the interior was first envisaged at the turn of the century, but it was not until 1954 that a Canadian-American treaty was signed and work was begun on the joint enterprise: the St Lawrence Seaway, which would provide navigation to a depth of twenty-seven feet from Montreal to the head of the Great Lakes and installations for the production of hydro-electric power. It is out of this latter development that Upper Canada Village grew.

The building of an enormous hydro dam at Cornwall was accompanied by the creation of a deep reservoir of water named Lake St Lawrence, a thirty-five-mile stretch of the river that today provides ocean-going ships with access to the Great Lakes and is capable of generating two million kilowatts of electricity. Unfortunately this great technological achievement required that, in Canada, seven villages and a third of the village of

Morrisburg had to be inundated and some sixty-five hundred people and more than five hundred houses relocated.

In many ways the region to be flooded was symbolic of the story of the birth and development of Ontario in the days when it was Upper Canada (and, after 1840, Canada West). Mostly farm land, it represented a large portion of the area first settled by the Loyalists in 1784. It was rich in history: it contained Crysler's Farm, the scene of one of the three decisive battles in the War of 1812, where on 11 November 1813 a small British-Canadian force defeated a numerically stronger American army. It also overlooked the picturesque and awesome Long Sault Rapids, one of the natural wonders of the St Lawrence River system.

To offset the loss of this highly significant area, the Province of Ontario established in 1955 the Ontario-St Lawrence Development Commission —predecessor of the present St Lawrence Parks

Commission—for the purpose of creating parklands along the St Lawrence with the objective that 'these lands are to be dedicated to the preservation of their historic past and to the education and recreational enjoyment of present and future generations'. The cornerstone of Commission policy was laid when it was decided to create a museum village. As the major part of the battlefield of Crysler's Farm was slated to disappear under twenty-eight feet of water, it was proposed that a memorial park be built and that it be located as close as possible to the site of the battlefield; the museum village would be the main feature of the park. And so it was that Upper Canada Village was created as part of Crysler's Farm Battlefield Park.

Working against time (the area was to be flooded in 1958), the Commission staff had to select the buildings that would be saved and have them moved to this new site. Initially it was thought that the Village should be created from the buildings, furnishings, equipment, and all material evidence of the period before 1867, that would be salvaged in the area to be flooded. It soon became evident, however, that if the Village was to represent various facets of life and endeavour from different times during the development of Upper Canada, the area of search would have to be expanded. Consequently structures and smaller artifacts were gathered from nine Loyalist counties on the St Lawrence—from Prince Edward County east to

(opposite) Aerial view of Upper Canada Village, showing its location on the river. In the lower right is Christ Church on Church Street and a few yards to the left is Cook's Tavern looking down Front Street, on which can be seen the French-Robertson House, Willard's Hotel, and Crysler Hall, with its grounds—all facing the river. The canal is a modern construction, as is the blockhouse (with its signalling mast) in the upper right, which represents a military telegraph station modelled on one used at Kingston during the War of 1812.

the Quebec border. In cases where a desired building type could not be found—a cheese factory, for example—a historical representation, faithfully constructed and equipped, was used.

Actual work on the site began in 1956 and was completed, in the main, by 1961. The task was both arduous and fascinating. The exact workings of old machinery, forgotten building techniques, hand-craft processes, and all the minutiae of life in the first half of the nineteenth century were examined with fine precision, an undertaking that required going beneath the surface of general history and engaging in detailed research. In the work of restoration, buildings were dissected to ascertain what was original under layers of paint and paper and what was alteration and addition. Home and business records had to be scrutinized to discover what items were available at the time, and then thousands of artifacts had to be found, repaired, and refurbished before being put in the households and shops of the Village to make them functional. Finally the artisans employed to reconstruct the Village had to be trained in the building practices of the nineteenth century.

From the first the planning and execution phases were entwined. On the executive side, setting broad policy and giving general direction, were the Commission chairman and general manager of the project, George Challies, and two vice-chairmen: Dr John Carroll and James Smart.

These three men, all of whom resided in the area, were also able to contribute much local knowledge. And it is undoubtedly true that without their close ties with the premier of the province, Leslie Frost, the project would not have been supported politically or financially. In charge of work on the site was a team formed by Professor Anthony Adamson of the School of Architecture, University of Toronto, who acted as a consultant; and—devoting full time to the project—Ronald Way, restorer and director of Old Fort Henry, assisted by Beryl Way; the architect Peter Stokes, who became a specialist in restoration; and Jeanne Minhinnick, a student of period furnishing. There was also an Advisory Board made up of Verschoyle Blake, Marion MacRae, and Philip Shackleton.

The Village is composed of individual historic units—including seven commercial and three industrial buildings, eleven houses, two churches, and a schoolhouse—each chosen to portray a segment of the social history of the region in the decades before Confederation. It acts as a time-machine, transporting visitors away from asphalt roads, automobiles, electricity, television, and the bustle of urban life. It beckons them through a toll gate, along a plank road into a world where farming was the main occupation, the horse was king, and there was no income tax. Costumed 'interpreters', who also carry out daily chores, bring it to life. Many of them are descendants of the original U.E.L. settlers and they remember their ancestors with feelings of sympathy and pride. Their welcome to visitors is genuine, for they do not find it difficult to think of the Village as their ancestral 'home'.*

Home life is central to Upper Canada Village. Indeed, in the nineteenth century businesses in rural communities were often carried on in the home. For instance, most taverns and hotels in Upper Canada—like Cook's Tavern (plate 36), at the centre of the Village—were private dwellings in which one or two rooms were set aside for the use of guests. This particular riverfront tavern was the focal point of community life—the stopping place for the stagecoach, and the bateaux that plied the river.

Michael Cook, a Loyalist from the Mohawk Valley, settled about a mile west of the Village and first took out a vendor's licence in 1804. His tavern achieved a notoriety of sorts during the War of 1812, when it served as the headquarters of General Wilkinson of the U.S. Army during the Battle of Crysler's Farm. After the war, with compensation received from the War Losses Act, Cook was able to build a new tavern-home, and it was this handsome red-brick Georgian building that was

*The Village is open from mid-May until mid-October.

Christ Church, from the French-Robertson House.

moved intact to Upper Canada Village. With its bar-room, commodious kitchen, and second-floor ballroom, it reflects the busy atmosphere of an establishment that provided meals and accommodation for travellers and was also the scene of political meetings, hearings of the magistrate's court, concerts, and dances.

The tavern, however, was not the only gathering-place in the community. The church was also important. Religion played a large part in peoples' lives from the cradle to the grave, and many of the political squabbles in Upper Canada in the first half of the nineteenth century could be laid at its door. The Rebellion of 1837 and the struggle for responsible government were linked to the attempt of the 'Family Compact' to extend special privileges to the Church of England— though in Upper Canada, Anglicans were in the minority; the Methodists were much more numerous.

Christ Church (plate 44), belonging to the Church of England, originally stood in Moulinette. Built in the Gothic style in 1837, before the Oxford movement made the use of chancels, high altars, and other 'Catholic' decoration stylish, it reflects the severe Puritan strain that was common in Protestant Upper Canada.

The Pastor's House (plate 47) was built in 1843 for the Reverend William Sharts, minister to the Lutheran congregation of Williamsburg Township, Dundas County. Since many of the Loyalists in this area were of German descent, Lutheranism was the first denomination in the county to establish a congregation complete with clergyman and church. The furnishings of the house reflect the Germanic background of its occupants.

During the early part of the nineteenth century many schools in Upper Canada were 'private', based in the teacher's home. The education provided was rather elementary—restricted to the three R's—though a few teachers, employed by the well-to-do, were equipped to provide a liberal education. The legislature passed the Grammar School Act of 1807 and the Common School Act of 1816, but school grants were so small that free education was impossible. Public education did not come into force until the 1840s and 1850s when, as a result of the work of Egerton Ryerson, a series of school acts brought into law a system of education that became recognized as one of the world's best. Education became possible for all, and throughout Upper Canada, regardless of the remoteness of the area, hundreds of schoolhouses sprang up. This period of prolific growth in education was immortalized by Ralph Connor in *Glengarry School Days* (1902), a novel that drew upon his youth in Athol, Glengarry County. The Schoolhouse in the Village (plate 60) is a reconstruction based on the school in his story.

The rural society of which Ralph Connor wrote

reached its zenith at the time of Confederation. Agriculture was Upper Canada's largest industry, providing a livelihood for most people and for many the only means of survival. For the new arrival in the bush, agriculture took the form of backbreaking toil to clear the land, to harvest the ashes produced by burning the forest, and to plant simple crops. Later, as more land was cleared, wheat became the staple crop. Not only was it easy to grow in the virgin land, but it was easily transported when converted into flour or whisky. Finally, about the time of the American Civil War, mixed farming became the key to prosperity. A combination of improved breeds of livestock and better horse-powered machinery—ploughs, reapers, and threshers—made it easier to provide sufficient animal food to last over the winter. As a result, milk production increased, and this led to the introduction of the cheese factory in 1864. Not long after, eastern Ontario became a world producer of cheddar cheese, and for the first time in Canadian history agricultural exports topped those of wood products. The established farmer became prosperous, as the farm house of John Loucks, J.P., U.E. (plate 53) shows.

In Upper Canada Village farming is carried on in every open space, and gardening around every house. Gardening was practised by almost everyone. It was mainly of the utilitarian variety, with vegetables and herbs the mainstay; decorative plantings amounted to little more than a few simple clumps of perennials or a small bed of annuals. Only the well-to-do, like John Pliny Crysler,* could hire the gardeners necessary to look after extensive lawns and flower beds. To keep roaming animals out and farm animals in, town lots were divided by board, picket, or cast-iron fences; farms by split-rail fences. In the Village there are at least ten different kinds of fences—one of the marks of a settled community.

While Upper Canada remained predominantly agricultural, industry entered the region gradually. The number of grist- and saw-mills increased steadily after 1784 as a result of the unlimited sources of water power. Most were small one-family operations, like the Heckston sawmill (see plates 9-11), and were run for only a few months a year. As the century wore on, larger mills or factories, employing many hands, were built. Even in rural areas small factories sprang up that reduced, little by little, the settlers' hand labour. By the 1860s the Asselstine Factory (plates 50-2), near Odessa, powered by a water turbine and using the latest machinery from Massachusetts, was turning out flannels, tweeds, blankets, and carpeting. While some women were still spinning and weaving their own cloth, more and more were using

*John Pliny Crysler (1801-81) was the son of John Crysler of Crysler's Farm. He built Crysler Hall (plate 71) about 1846 when he was a successful timber merchant.

factory cloth. The productivity of the 240 spindles on Michael Asselstine's spinning jack could not be compared to that of the single spindle on the spinning wheel. The Industrial Revolution was changing the face of Upper Canada.

The wealth a single person could derive from commerce and industry is reflected in the home of George Robertson (plate 18). He bought his house, a small timber-frame structure with brick-filled walls, from his father-in-law, Lieutenant Jeremiah French, late of the King's Royal Regiment of New York. Robertson enlarged and renovated it—adding Neo-Classical details to the exterior—in 1820. The house (sometimes called 'Maple Grove') contains a few pieces of his fine furniture, some of which was imported, some made locally. The original hand-blocked wallpaper in the parlour is still being admired a century and a half after he bought it.

Most of the tradesmen of the time—blacksmiths, wheelwrights, coopers, carpenters—engaged in the mundane but necessary tasks of building and repairing the essential objects of everyday life. Some artisans, however, such as the cabinetmaker, created beautiful as well as useful pieces that a hundred years later would be collectors' items. Indigenous woods—cherry, maple,

From the kitchen of the Doctor's House.

and walnut—were frequently combined by skilled craftsmen to produce furniture every bit as fine as that made in London or New York. The Village cabinetmaker carries on this tradition (plate 31).

'Tradition' is one of the key words at Upper Canada Village. Others are authenticity, heritage, preservation, and education. The purpose of the Village is to preserve, study, and interpret the historical resources of the counties of eastern Ontario settled by the United Empire Loyalists. It is accomplishing this goal by collecting significant artifacts, documenting and testing them for historical worth, and displaying them for visitors so that they may receive some inspiration and enjoyment from their heritage.

After twenty years the Village has a settled look; it has put down roots. The scars of relocated buildings and trees, the signs of new construction, and the changes in the terrain wrought by great earth-moving machines are no longer visible. Mother Nature has healed the surgical wounds of creation and Upper Canada Village exists serenely in its setting, bringing to life a quiet farming area of a century and a half ago—with only modern ocean-going vessels sailing by to remind us of the twentieth century.

1 Sunrise at Upper Canada Village, from the canal.

2 Summer ploughing in a field next to the Pastor's House.

3   The stagecoach, which carried passengers and mail. The heyday
of the stagecoach in Upper Canada was the 1830s and 1840s.

4 *(left)* Coiling hay.

5 Backing a load of hay into the barn.

BAKERY

6 Loaves of whole-wheat bread.

7 & 8 *(right)* Setting off on a delivery.

SAWMILL AREA

9　*(left)* Making an axe handle.

10　Cutting a log into boards.

11　The logs behind the axeman will
be squared like the log in the foreground.

BLACKSMITH'S SHOP

12   A rack like this held an ox while it was being shod to enable it to walk on macadamized roads. The animal had to be partly supported during the operation because an ox cannot stand on three legs.

13   *(right)* Oxen pulling a farm wagon.

14 *(left)* The driveshed behind Willard's Hotel.

15 A farmer's market wagon.

16 *(left)* Picking currants.

17 Purple loosestrife.

FRENCH-ROBERTSON HOUSE

18 *(left)* A prosperous merchant's dwelling of Georgian simplicity and elegance, it was built by Jeremiah French in 1784 and enlarged in 1820 by his son-in-law, George Robertson, who applied the Neo-Classical detailing to the façade. It was moved from Mille Roches, Stormont County, and restored to 1820. The cheerful fence, with its urn-topped posts, is a reconstruction based on an old photograph of a contemporary fence in Iroquois, Ont.

19 The entrance door, with Doric pilasters; its decorative moulding—a double swag with pendant husks—is associated with interiors.

FRENCH-ROBERTSON HOUSE

20 & 21 Interior, looking from the kitchen into the bedrooms
(plate 20), the first of which is the subject of plate 21.

CRYSLER HALL

22 & 23 Two views of the orna-
mental flower garden. The
cast-iron fence, which was not
originally associated with Crysler
Hall, dates from the 1850s.
(See also plate 71).

24 Making an apple pie in the kitchen of the Schoolmaster's House.

25 *(right)* Dipping candles in the summer kitchen of the Farm House.

26 Spinning wool.

27 Skeins of spun wool, with some carded (unspun) wool on the left.

28 *(right)* Skeins of wool dyed with natural dyes.

HIRED MAN'S HOUSE

32 Upstairs bedroom.

33 Parlour.

34 *(right)* Exterior.

35 Walking past the French-Robertson fence towards Cook's Tavern.

36 *(right)* COOK'S TAVERN. The French-Robertson House is on the right.

COOK'S TAVERN

37 Dining room.

38 Ballroom. The bed on the right is a settle-bed—a pull-out
bed for an extra guest.

39 *(left)* Walking to the store.

40 Looking out a window of the Woollen Mill at a replica
of an 1850s general store.

41 & 42   Out for a walk.

CHRIST CHURCH

43 Interior.

44 *(right)* Exterior. This white frame church in the Picturesque Gothic style,
built in 1837, was the gift to his community of Adam Dixson, a mill owner
of Moulinette, Stormont County. (He did not live to see it completed.)
The largest structure to be moved to the Village, it was restored to 1837.

45 *(overleaf)* The church in late afternoon,
from the Common. The Pastor's House is on the left.

PASTOR'S HOUSE

46 *(left)* The parlour.

47 Exterior. This frame house was built in 1843. Moved from the riverfront, Williamsburg Township, Dundas County, it was restored to 1845.

PROVIDENCE CHURCH

48 *(left)* Interior. The pulpit is
original but the pews, though in
period, came from another
church.

49 Exterior. Providence Church
was built c.1845. Moved from
Crystal, Leeds County, it was
restored to 1845. It was used by
several denominations, mostly
Methodists. (The chimney is
covered for the winter.)

ASSELSTINE FACTORY

50 *(left)* A distant view of the Woollen Mill across the millpond. Build c.1840, it was moved from Mill Creek, Lennox and Addington Counties, and restored to 1867.

51 Full bobbins, with a blanket warp in the background.

52 Looking through 240 threads being spun on a spinning jack, with a basket of empty bobbins in the foreground and spools of unspun wool in the background.

FARM HOUSE

53   Exterior. This stone house was built by John Loucks in 1846.
Moved from the riverfront, Osnabruck Township, Stormont
County, it was restored to the 1860s.

54 The parlour.

55   FARM HOUSE: bedroom.

56 FARM HOUSE: diningroom.

57 *(left)* CHEESE FACTORY. A historical representation to 1867.

58 The back of the Cook's Tavern barn from the canal, showing the stern of the Village bateau, the *Marguerite* (a reconstruction).

SCHOOLHOUSE

59 Moved from Athol, Glengarry County, this log building was altered to the 1860s to resemble the school that Ralph Connor described in *Glengarry Schooldays*.

60 *(right)* Front view.

ROSS-BOFFIN HOUSE

61 *(left)* Built c.1810. Moved from the riverfront, Lancaster Township, Glengarry County, it was restored to 1810. This single-room log house—one of several squared-timber buildings in the Village—boasts a harmoniously proportioned Georgian exterior.

62 Quilting inside the Ross-Boffin House.

63   A stook of oats, with the steeple of Christ Church in the background.

64   *(right)* Sheep on the canal berm.

65   *(left)* WILLARD'S HOTEL. Built c.1795. Moved from
the riverfront of Williamsburg Township, Dundas
County, it was restored to 1850.

66   DOCTOR'S HOUSE. Built in 1845. Moved from the
village of Aultsville, Stormont County, it was restored
to 1850.

67 MCDIARMID HOUSE. Built c.1860. Moved from Sandringham, Stormont County, it was restored to 1860.

68 CRYSLER'S STORE. Built
c.1820. Moved from the riverfront, Williamsburg Township,
Dundas County, it was rebuilt and
furnished as a store of the 1860s.
This building belonged to John
Pliny Crysler of Crysler Hall.

69 & 70 CRYSLER'S STORE: interior. The large object in the foreground of plate 70 is a coffee mill.

71 *(overleaf)* CRYSLER HALL. Built c.1846 and moved from the riverfront, Williamsburg Township, Dundas County. The handsome portico, with pediment and Doric columns, suggests a temple, in the American Classical Revival style. This imposing exterior was restored to 1846. (The interior is now a museum.) The impressive effect is completed by a circular drive and formal garden.

72   The Village late on an autumn afternoon. The bateau is in a
lock, in front of the raised footbridge. Christ Church can be seen
in the background.